Herbal Teas

Herbal Teas

Richard Craze

AN IMPRINT OF RUNNING PRESS
PHILADELPHIA • LONDON

A QUINTET BOOK

9 8 7 6 5 4 3 2 1

Digit on the right indicates the number of this printing

ISBN 0-7624-0103-6

Library of Congress
Cataloguing-in-Publication Number 97-68288

This book was designed and produced by
Quintet Publishing Limited
6 Blundell Street
London N7 9BH

Creative Director: Richard Dewing
Art Director: Silke Braun
Designer: Isobel Gillan
Senior Editor: Sally Green
Editors: Jane Hurd-Cosgrave, Janette Marshall
Photographer: Tim Ferguson-Hill
Food Stylist: Kathryn Hawkins

Typeset in Great Britain by
Central Southern Typesetters, Eastbourne
Manufactured in Singapore by Eray Scan Pte Ltd.

Published by Courage Books, and imprint of
Running Press Book Publishers
125 South Twenty-Second Street
Philadelphia, Pennsylvania 19103-4399

This book is not intended as a substitute for the advice of a
health care professional. Any herbs with a strong action should be avoided during pregnancy.
The reader should regularly consult a health care practitioner in matters relating to health, particularly
with respect to any symptoms that may require diagnosis or medical attention.
Do not take any herbal remedies if you are currently under any medication without first checking with a
doctor or other qualified medical personnel.

Contents

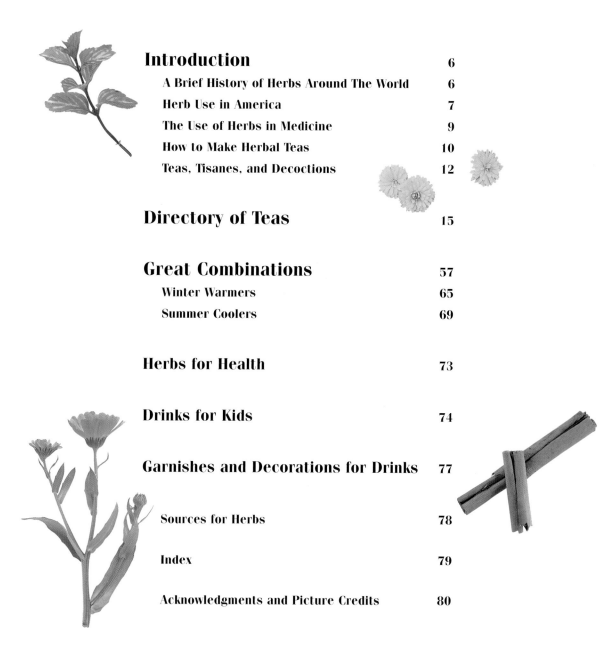

Introduction

Herbs are the fragrant flowers, leaves, stems, roots, and seeds of various green plants from around the world. They can either be found growing wild or especially cultivated for human consumption, usually in gardens or on larger, commercial farms. Because most herbaceous plants do not become persistent, but die down to the ground—or entirely—after flowering, this makes them naturally both easier to use and more generally available in their dried form, although many consider that they are best used when fresh for cooking and producing fragrant products.

A Brief History of Herbs
Around the World

The resurgent popularity of herb growing and interest in their use for medical, culinary, and cosmetic purposes is predated by an extensive and fascinating history, stretching as far back as man's earliest ancestors. For example, an archeological dig at a 60,000-year-old Neanderthal site contained evidence of the use of marshmallow, yarrow, and groundsel—all herbs that are still used today. An ancient Middle Eastern papyrus text believed to have originated in the 16th century, B.C. features recipes with references to the medicinal properties of over 700 herbs, including wormwood, peppermint, myrrh, aloe, henbane, and castor oil—and even recommends using the mold (later discovered as the source of penicillin) found on bread to treat wounds and prevent infection. There are also numerous references to herbs in the Bible, and many Greek and Roman writers, including Hippocrates, "the Father of Medicine," Theophrastus (372–287 B.C.), Discorides (1st century, A.D.), author of the Latin *De Materica Medica*, Pliny the Elder, and Galen, compiled detailed analyses of plants and their proper usage. After the demise of the Roman Empire, herbal knowledge was largely passed on throughout Europe by Christian monks, and by word of mouth through lay communities and medical practitioners. Seven hundred years ago, foxglove was prescribed by medieval European physicians to patients suffering from chest pains and heart trouble, and it is now recognized that its active ingredient, digitalis, is a potent cardiotonic.

During the Age of Exploration, in which Europeans made their great sea voyages to foreign lands, the ancient herb lore and wisdom practiced and passed on by oral tradition in other cultures began to be written down and available, and the knowledge of the range of herbal benefits from around the world was increased. The ancient Aztec emperors had encouraged their people to learn all about the varieties of plants in their regions, and when Cortez and the conquistadors invaded Mexico in the 1500s, they discovered a people rich in herbal knowledge. When word of these amazing plants reached King Philip II of Spain, he sent his personal physician to catalog and describe the Aztec plants. A Mexican Indian doctor, Juan Badianus, provided the first written record of native American herb lore and medical practices in 1552. Voyages to India and China also brought the first contact with ancient Indian

15th-century herb and flower garden, from The Playfair Book of Hours, French illuminated manuscript.

Ayurvedic medicinal traditions and Chinese herbal remedies, which extended back in written form to 2500 B.C. with the work of Huang Ti, the Yellow Emperor, who knew so much about herbal medicine that he invented writing just so that he could record all of his knowledge; it is still regarded as one of the foremost works on herbal medicine. Li Shizen, a famous 16th-century Chinese naturalist, also compiled an encyclopedia describing nearly 2,000 medicines and 11,000 herbal prescriptions. European contact with India and China developed the fashion for drinking tea, and the trade in spices and herbs from these countries became quite lucrative.

Herb use *in America*

Meanwhile, English writers in the 16th and 17th centuries, such as John Gerald, John Parkinson, and Nicholas Culpeper, were compiling herbal manuals, each extending the amount of information that had previously been available through the ancient Greek, Roman, and medieval European traditions. Culpeper's herbal (as these works were called), *The English Physician*, published in

1652, was one of the most famous herbal manuals, although it was often discredited as quackery because of its numerous references to astrology. The early American colonists took these books with them to the New World, also importing many herbs, fruit trees, vegetables, and various flowering bulbs from the Old World to maintain their households. However, they also soon discovered that the Native American peoples they encountered had a vast storehouse of knowledge regarding medicinal properties of indigenous American plants, and through this exchange, the early settlers learned about the use of herbs in healing wounds, safe childbirth practices, and setting fractures. The apprentice medicine men of the Chippewa Nation were extensively educated in various plants, and specialized in one disease or related diseases; we owe to them our knowledge of many indigenous herbs in use today, such as *Cascara sagrada*, American ginseng, joe pye-weed, goldenseal, yellow dock, burdock, sarsparilla, sassafras (the main ingredient in root beer), and witch hazel. The Seminole Indians along the southeast coastal states used to grow water hyacinths to clear fouled swamp water, and today we know that these can be used to limit water pollution. This two-way exchange of information during the first hundred years of settlement was chronicled by many fascinating contemporary accounts, most notably by the Winthrop family and John Josselyn, an English naturalist who voyaged back and forth during the 17th century.

The events of the Boston Tea Party in 1773, when colonial settlers disguised as Native Americans threw the imported tea cargoes from English ships into the harbor in reaction to the severe taxes imposed on the goods by King George III's government, have possibly contributed to the American preference for coffee. In the past 200 years, some of the taste for tea was restored, with ice tea in particular being a popular U.S. beverage. Herb use in general was in decline throughout the 19th century, apart from the Shakers, whose religious beliefs and regard for simplicity led them to cultivate herbs widely for a variety

of purposes. But the new strides made in the development of synthetic medicines meant that herbs were no longer the chief source of medicinal treatment, and many people stopped growing them as they were no longer needed to preserve foods with the advent of new technologies. However, as more and more Americans are today searching for "healthier" alternatives to caffeinated drinks such as tea and coffee, herbal teas of all descriptions have become increasingly popular, and there is a renewed respect for their contribution to alternative or complementary medicinal treatments.

The Use of Herbs in Medicine

Current medical research confirms that many herbs used for centuries by the ancient Chinese, Indian, European, Aboriginal, and Native American peoples to treat illnesses can provide a solid, scientifically proven "cure" or basis for treatment—in fact, nearly 30 percent of the drugs commonly used and prescribed today are either derived from a plant source or contain chemical imitations of a plant compound, including aspirin (derived from the bark of the white willow tree), reserpine (a blood pressure medicine made from an ancient Indian remedy derived from an Asian shrub), ephedrine and pseudoephedrine (derived from Ma Huang, or the ephedra plant, used in China for over 5,000 years to treat colds and flus), valium (derived from the valerian root), vincristine and vinblastine (used to treat childhood leukemia, and derived from the rosy periwinkle tree), and quinine and quinidine (used to treat malaria and as an anti-arrhythmic medication, made from the bark of the cinchona tree). Many indigenous peoples with an incredible longevity attribute their enduring good health to the use of such herbs, among other dietary components. With such evidence of their medicinal value, it is no wonder that many people around the world have rediscovered herbs.

Herbs are quickly rehydrated to make herbal teas.

Being mostly dried for ease of storage and transportation, herbs are easily and quickly rehydrated in hot water to make herbal teas. These *tisanes*, or teas, have traditionally been drunk to increase the appetite, lubricate the intestines, increase resistance to infection, improve circulation, promote perspiration, soothe inflammation, and to strengthen the blood, bones, and tissues, as well as being gentle and natural laxatives. Herbs have antibacterial and disinfectant qualities, and the alkaloids they contain stimulate our glands—which in turn regulate our levels of energy, nerves, fitness, and aging. All in all, not a bad list of achievements for something as simple and easy to prepare as a cup of tea! In *Herbal Teas* we will examine and explore how to make our own herbal teas using some of the most common and easily grown herbs to treat simple conditions. However, for any conditions of a serious nature, we would recommend that you consult a qualified medical practitioner immediately. In Chinese herbal medicine, drastic conditions such as appendicitis may be treated with herbal prescriptions, but we cannot recommend this. We suggest that the only conditions you treat with herbal teas are ones that would normally be treated with ordinary, nonprescription remedies bought from a drugstore.

OTHER USES FOR HERBS

Herbs have also traditionally been used as insecticides; in pot pourri and herb pillows; for incense and candle making; for cosmetics, including herbal baths, face packs, skin fresheners, lotions, creams, and moisturizers, as well as perfumes, shampoos, and dyes; for first-aid, including cuts, sprains, insect stings, warts, boils, and pain relief. And herbs are, of course, also used to flavor, preserve,

Herbs are mostly dried for ease of storage and transportation.

and color food. However, the most common use of herbs is in the preparation of herbal teas, as prescribed to relieve a variety of ailments.

How to Make Herbal Teas

Before you can make a herbal tea, you have to obtain the proper herbs. These can be bought already dried from health-food shops, specialist grocers, and stores, mail order catalogs (see Stockists, page 78), and even on the Internet (see page 79). Fresh herbs are also available from supermarkets, garden centers, and ethnic grocery stores. Not all herbs are available commercially, and these you may wish to grow yourself.

Most of the herbs used in *Herbal Teas* grow in moderate climates, which makes them ideal growing in the garden in spring or summer. If you do not have a garden, many herbs will thrive outdoors in summer in pots and containers on window sills, balconies, conservatories, or indoors in the winter. The only

Herbs are ideal plants to grow in the garden.

drawbacks to growing herbs yourself is finding space to grow the quantity you need, and the restrictions of seasonality in harvesting flowers. Herbs planted in pots will last longer if you pick just a few leaves at a time as you need them.

If you want to dry herbs, the best way is to hang them up by their stems in a warm, dry place, such as the pantry. Put a tray or newspaper beneath to catch any seeds that fall. Some seeds may be ground for culinary use, or used as seed stock when replanting. Drying herbs in an oven is not recommended, as the herbs dry too quickly, and lose their essential oil.

WHAT'S IN A NAME?

Originally, tea was a generic word for any infusion with water, be it peppermint leaves to make peppermint tea, or beef bones to make beef tea. Today, "tea" usually refers to the drink made with leaves from the tea plants grown mainly in India, Sri Lanka, and China. Herbal teas refer to teas whose main ingredient is a herb. Some contain just one herb; others contain combinations of herbs, or herbs mixed with normal (caffeinated, Indian, or Chinese) tea to add the medicinal benefits found in herbs to the stimulant effects of caffeine.

There are no specific regulations that state what may or may not be used as an ingredient in a commercially produced herbal or fruit tea. But, having said that, tea is covered by the Food and Drugs Administration, which makes it illegal to sell any food or drink that is not safe to consume.

Pick just a few leaves at a time and your potted herbs will last longer.

Equipment

There is nothing complicated about making herbal teas. They can be made directly in the cup, or in a tea pot. The latter requires a tea strainer when pouring the herbal tea. Earthenware or china tea pots with plastic and nylon filter-baskets that lift out of the pot when the required strength has been reached are ideal. They allow better control over strength and flavor, and do not require a tea strainer when pouring. Glass coffee or tea pots that use the cafetière/plunger method are pretty, because you can see the tea, but they have the disadvantage of the herbs remaining in the water, which affects the flavor over time.

Teas, tisanes, and decoctions

Another name for herbal tea is "tisane," which is made by infusing fresh or dried herbs, usually leaves or flowers, in hot water. In general, a herbal tea, tisane, or infusion is made by pouring 2½ cups of hot, but not necessarily boiling water, over 1 teaspoon of dried or ½ to 1 ounce fresh herb, then leaving the herbs to infuse for a few minutes until the tea is cool enough to drink.

The flavor of herbal teas can vary from mild and subtle to strong and bitter. Herbal tea is usually drunk black, but you can flavor herbal teas with a little sugar or honey, milk, or slices of lemon, orange, or lime, if you prefer.

Herbs with a strong scent, such as peppermint and rosemary, contain a large amount of volatile oil, and should be infused in a closed container such as a tea pot to prevent losing the oils, as they contain the flavor and aroma. As a rule, flowers, leaves, and other delicate parts of the plant are infused, while the tougher parts, such as the roots, bark, and woody stems are decocted.

Decoctions are mainly used in herbal medicine. This method gets the essential ingredients out of the root, bark, or seeds, which should be chopped or bruised beforehand to help the process. In general, use 1 teaspoon of dried herbs or 1 tablespoon of fresh to 1 cup of cold water. Bring to a boil, and simmer for 20 minutes until the liquid has reduced by about two thirds. Steep (allowing to cool with the ingredients still in) until cool. Strain into a cup, and add honey or sugar to taste. A decoction should ideally be made fresh every day, but you can keep it in the refrigerator for two days, if necessary.

Warning
Any herbs with a strong action should be avoided during pregnancy. Do not take any herbal remedies if you are currently under any medication without first checking with a doctor or other qualified medical personnel.

1. Chop or bruise the root, bark, or seeds of the herbs and place in a saucepan. Pour on the required amount of water – 1 tsp dried herbs or 1 Tbsp fresh herbs to 1 cup of cold water.

2. Bring to a boil and simmer for 20 minutes until liquid has reduced by about ⅔. Steep until cool.

3. Strain the contents of the saucepan into your cup, tea pot, or chosen container for herbal tea.

> **For tips on the preparation of teas and decoctions for individual herbs, see the Directory of Teas, pages 14–61. Recipes are given on pages 62–77.**

To sweeten herbal tea, simply add sugar or honey to taste.

Terms

Some of the common herbal terms are as follows:

Demulcent—a substance in the herb that soothes the bronchials and eases coughing.

Expectorant—a herb that helps get rid of excess mucus in the lungs.

Diuretic—a herb that helps increase the flow of urine.

Astringent—these herbs tone up the mucous membranes.

Carminative—herbs to settle upset stomachs and dispel gas. They may also ease heartburn and colic.

Buying and Identifying Herbs

Herbs are quite safe if used correctly. There are a few guidelines you should follow, however. For example, each herb in the directory is listed under both its "common" and its Latin name to help identify them, but when buying or using herbs, you should identify them only from their Latin name. The common name can vary from country to country—and even within countries, each region may call the same plant by different names. For instance what is called pennyroyal in America (*Hedeoma pulegiodes*) is different from the European pennyroyal (*Mentha pulegium*), and different again from Australian pennyroyal (*Mentha saturioides*), although all three do have very similar properties. Always check the "Cautions" entry in the Directory of Teas before making up a new herbal tea.

Directory of teas

The directory consists of a user-friendly guide to the herbs available for use in herbal teas. You will find each entry contains the origin of the herb, its description and habitat, its uses, any scientific knowledge, the parts used in the making of the tea, the taste you can expect, and details of how to prepare it. The directory is listed alphabetically by common name. There are over 60 delicious teas to try, many of which are not only tasty and refreshing, but have health-enhancing properties too. Once you've discovered your favorites and have familiarized yourself with how to prepare them, you can experiment with the Great Combinations detailed in the following section.

Agrimony

Agrimonia eupatoria

In medieval times, agrimony was regarded as a cure-all, with near-magical powers. Its name derives from the Greek word "agremone," meaning plants with an ability to heal eye disorders. It is also known as "church steeples." It is of European origin, but now grows profusely throughout the United States, where it was introduced by the early settlers.

DESCRIPTION AND HABITAT

A perennial growing up to 2 feet high, with small, yellow flowers topping tall, tapering spikes. The leaves are as hairy as the stems. It is sweet-smelling, and grows just about everywhere in Europe and North America.

USES

Taken as a tea, it is said to be a general tonic and digestive aid, and is traditionally used for bladder complaints such as cystitis, also gallstones, and cirrhosis of the liver. Its diuretic properties are used for treating gout. As a mouthwash, it is used for mouth ulcers and inflamed gums.

SCIENTIFIC KNOWLEDGE

Research has shown agrimony to increase the coagulation of the blood by up to 50 percent. Widely used for a number of treatments in traditional Asian herbal medicine.

PARTS USED

The leaves, flowers, and juice.

TASTE

A delicate scent and flavor.

PREPARATION

Pick and dry the leaves just before the plant flowers, and use the leaves in an infusion. Agrimony with dandelion is a traditional herbal tea remedy for arthritis.

CAUTIONS

No known side effects.

Angelica

Angelica archangelica

Angelica originated in Europe, where the traditional lore tells the story of how it was named for an angel who revealed its healing properties to a priest, claiming that it was a cure for the plague. It was once known as the Root of the Holy Ghost.

DESCRIPTION AND HABITAT

This plant can grow to over 7 feet high and is very common throughout Europe, Asia, and North America. It has large, green leaves and a thick, hollow stem. The flowers are small and green/yellow.

USES

Infused as a tea, it is taken traditionally to stimulate the circulation and help digestion. It is

also used as a diuretic and antiseptic, and for treating painful periods; it hastens menstruation through its antispasmodic action. The cold tea can be used as an eye bath for sore and strained eyes. The flavor of jams and marmalades benefit from the addition of a little chopped stem. The leaves can be used to flavor fish stews, and the stem is often candied and used to decorate cakes.

SCIENTIFIC KNOWLEDGE

It is a recognized antifungal agent.

PARTS USED

The stem, leaves, seeds, and root.

TASTE

Sweet at first, but can then taste sharp and bitter. Infused, dried leaves used in a tea can taste like a Chinese tea.

PREPARATION

The tea can be made by infusing either root, seeds, or leaves in boiling water.

CAUTIONS

Angelica has high sugar content, so diabetics should be careful. Take only infrequently, as it can overstimulate and cause insomnia.

Aniseed

Pimpinella anisum

A Mediterranean plant that has been used at least since Roman times. Early colonists carried the seed to North America, where Shakers grew it in their medicinal herb crops. The whole plant smells fragrant, and the sweet-tasting, licorice-like seeds, when chewed, help to improve the appetite and aid digestion. The root of a similarly flavored, U.S.-native plant, anise hyssop (*Agastache foeniculum*), was used in Cree and Chippewa teas for lung problems.

DESCRIPTION AND HABITAT
Aniseed grows in the wild, but can be easily cultivated in any moderately warm climate. It grows about 18 inches high, and has broad leaves, with small, creamy flowers. The seeds are light brown and hairy.

USES
The seeds are chewed after meals to aid digestion and sweeten the breath. The fresh leaves can be used to flavor curries and spicy meat dishes. The oil is used in toothpaste. Aniseed tea, in combination with fennel and caraway, is useful in settling upset stomachs and as a colic remedy.

SCIENTIFIC KNOWLEDGE
Anise oil helps to relieve stomach cramps. Its principle ingredient is anethole, which is used in the manufacture of insect repellents and cough medicines.

PARTS USED
The leaves, oil, and seeds.

TASTE
Similar to fennel; both spicy and sweet. The leaves are more delicate.

PREPARATION
To make aniseed tea, either infuse the fresh leaves or use 1 teaspoon of crushed seeds steeped in hot water for 10 minutes. Strain before using, and sip slowly.

CAUTIONS
Not to be confused with Japanese star anise, which is poisonous.

Basil

Ocimum basilicum

Also known as St. Joseph wort, garden basil, rubin basil, and sweet basil. It grows almost anywhere from Egypt to North America, although it originates in India, where it is regarded as sacred. It is often seen in pots outside houses in hot countries, where it is used to repel insects. It is an important ingredient in pesto.

DESCRIPTION AND HABITAT
Basil can be cultivated in gardens or grown in pots as a useful culinary herb. It grows to a maximum height of 2 feet, with broad leaves and spiky, creamy/white flowers. Basil is now cultivated in many leaf varieties that range from white to purple. There is a lemon-scented basil, a purple basil-lettuce, and a bush basil.

USES

Basil is a useful culinary herb, widely used in Mediterranean dishes, and especially complementary to tomatoes and garlic. The fresh leaves should only be added towards the end of the cooking to preserve the flavor. Medical herbalists use basil as an antispasmodic, to aid digestion, settle the stomach, and relieve nausea.

SCIENTIFIC KNOWLEDGE
Basil contains an essential oil—estragol—which is used in insect repellent manufacture.

PARTS USED
The leaves, fresh and dried.

TASTE
Similar to thyme. The leaves have a minty flavor when dried.

PREPARATION
Infuse 2 teaspoons of the dried leaves in 1 cup of hot water to make a tea for settling the stomach. Honey can be added to make a tea for relieving tickly coughs and clearing catarrh.

CAUTIONS
No known side effects.

Bergamot/ *Bee balm*

Monarda didyma

Also known as Oswego tea and Indian plume. Wild bergamot is a native of North America that was used as a tea by the Oswego Indians to cure colds, later becoming a popular replacement for tea in New England after the Boston Tea Party. It was named for Dr. Nicholas Monardes, the Spanish botanist who wrote his herbal on American flora in 1569. He called it "bergamot" because the leaves smell similar to Italian bergamot oranges.

DESCRIPTION AND HABITAT

It grows to 3 feet high, with downy leaves and creamy flowers in the spring followed by long, dark fruit. The fragrance of the whole plant is reminiscent of licorice and aniseed.

USES

Fresh leaves may be added to salads, summer drinks, or stuffings. Dried, it makes a tea, and the oil can be used for skin conditions. Traditionally used to relieve menstrual pains, insomnia, gas, and nausea.

SCIENTIFIC KNOWLEDGE

Bergamot has proven antiseptic, diaphoretic (promotes perspiration), and anesthetic properties.

PARTS USED

The leaves and flowers.

TASTE

Pleasant, lemony, perfumed.

PREPARATION

To make a nightcap, use 1 tablespoon of dried, shredded leaves and pour over 1¼ cups of hot milk. Allow to stand for 1 to 2 minutes then strain. To make a tea, simmer 1 teaspoon of dried bergamot in 1 cup of water for 10 minutes.

CAUTIONS

No known side effects.

Betony

Stachys officinalis

An ancient European herb formerly used as a dye and medicine. In medieval times, it was considered able to ward off evil spirits, and was commonly planted in country churchyards for this reason—which is how it got its other name of bishopwort. The fresh plant yields a yellow dye, which can be used as a shampoo to tint gray hair.

DESCRIPTION AND HABITAT

Grows wild in Europe to a height of about 20 inches, and has dark leaves with red/purple flowers.

USES

Betony is commonly used as an ingredient in the manufacture of medicines for digestive disorders and rheumatic conditions. The juice of the plant can be applied externally to ulcers and cuts, while the tea is said to be effective, if taken regularly, against varicose veins.

SCIENTIFIC KNOWLEDGE

Betony contains tannins and alkaloids that act as digestive stimulants and sedatives. It is used in the treatment of menopausal problems.

PARTS USED

Use the leaves dried for an infusion, and fresh for a poultice.

TASTE

Betony has a mild, pleasant, delicate taste, a bit like a fragrant Chinese tea.

PREPARATION

Add 1 to 2 teaspoons of dried leaves to 1 cup of hot water, and use only once or twice a day (see *Cautions*). The tea can be used as a tonic for headaches or as a replacement for Indian teas.

CAUTIONS

The root or fresh leaves should not be taken internally, as they contain a bitter, astringent oil. Do not take betony during pregnancy. If taken in excess, betony can cause vomiting and diarrhea.

Blackberry

Rubus fruticosus, R. villosus

The blackberry goes by many other names, including bramble, cloudberry, dewberry, and goutberry. The last gives a clue to its traditional medicinal properties.

DESCRIPTION AND HABITAT

Almost any moderate climate will support the blackberry's growth. It usually grows in the wild, around the edges of woods. It is probably best known for its sharp thorns, although some cultivated varieties have lost these. The flowers are tiny and white, and the fruit is often used in desserts and jellies.

USES

The fruit is used in culinary preparations. The leaves are dried and made into tea, said to be especially effective in combating gout, or chewed fresh, which is said to help bleeding gums. Also used to combat digestive disorders, especially diarrhea.

SCIENTIFIC KNOWLEDGE

Blackberry has an astringent effect, which is known to contract tissue and reduce secretions.

PARTS USED

The root, leaves (dried and fresh), and fruit.

TASTE

The fruit is sharp and sweet, while the leaves are milder but still tangy.

PREPARATION

For a herbal tea, use 4 teaspoons of dried leaves to 1 cup of hot water. The fresh leaves can be used in a decoction to produce a herbal remedy for gout and asthma.

CAUTIONS

No known side effects.

Caraway

Carum carvi

Also known as St. Joseph wort, Caraway originated in the Middle East, and it has been grown as a herb for at least 5,000 years—the Egyptians buried their dead with it, and remains of caraway have been found in Stone Age settlements. The ancient folklore surrounding this herb imbued it with magical properties; it was said to give protection from witches and prevent departures, and was therefore a frequent ingredient in love potions.

DESCRIPTION AND HABITAT

Grows wild throughout Europe, and some of the cooler Asian countries. It is cultivated on a large scale in The Netherlands and Russia. It has bright green leaves, and grows to around 8 inches high.

USES

Mostly culinary, as a flavoring for cakes and breads. Medicinally, it may aid digestion. Chewing the seeds can also sweeten the breath. A strong infusion can be used as a gargle to ease sore throats.

SCIENTIFIC KNOWLEDGE

In the pharmaceutical trade, caraway is often added to laxatives to reduce their unpleasant effects, and to various other products that treat digestive problems.

PARTS USED

The stems, leaves, seeds, and oil. The roots can be cooked and used as a vegetable, as they have a similar taste to parsnips. The leaves can be used like parsley, as a garnish in salads.

TASTE

Aromatic, warming.

PREPARATION

Use 6 teaspoons of crushed seeds to 1 cup of hot water. As a decoction, use 6 teaspoons of seeds, then boil in 1 cup of milk and leave to steep for 10 minutes. The decoction, when taken cool, may relieve colic in children and ease gas and reduce menstrual cramps in adults.

CAUTIONS

No known side effects.

USES

Widely known as a salad ingredient, the stems can be chopped and added to soups, stews, and meat dishes. The aromatic seeds are also be added to casseroles and stews. Herbalists use celery as a digestive and stimulant, to lower blood pressure, and to treat heartburn and rheumatism.

SCIENTIFIC KNOWLEDGE

Proven to relieve symptoms of osteo- and rheumatoid arthritis. Celery is a diuretic and has anti-inflammatory properties.

PARTS USED

The root, seeds, stem, and leaves.

TASTE

Sharp, fresh. Warming when cooked.

PREPARATION

Grind 1 teaspoon of seeds, and add up to 1 cup of hot water. Let stand for 10 minutes, and drink while still warm. The juice of celery stalk can be extracted in a food processor and drunk when cool.

CAUTIONS

Avoid the juice if high blood pressure is diagnosed, as celery has a high sodium content. Wild celery should not be consumed during pregnancy.

Celery/ Smallage

Apium graveolens var. dulce.

A native of Mediterranean countries, celery leaves and stems were originally used by the Greeks and Romans for medicinal and culinary purposes, but it was not until the Italian cultivated variety was introduced in the 1700s that it was utilized as a vegetable. The Shakers grew celery for their nostrums and other medicinal compounds, and it later became a popular American salad ingredient.

DESCRIPTION AND HABITAT

The leaves are yellow/green. It has a thick, juicy stem and white flowers.

Chamomile

Anthemis nobilis

A European native; also called whig plant, ground apple, and garden chamomile. There are many different species of chamomile, and the best for tea is the Italian (*Anthemis nobilis*) or German (*Matricaria chamomilla*) chamomile. Its sweet-scented leaves have traditional associations with health, tranquility, and beauty—in addition to being frequently prescribed as a cure for insomnia or to reduce tension, chamomile tea is often served in beauty parlors to help relax facial muscles. Chamomile is probably best known for its strong, calming effect.

DESCRIPTION AND HABITAT

It has fine leaves with daisy-like flowers, and grows only 8 to 10 inches above ground.

USES

The flowers, when soaked in hot water, strained, and wrapped in a cloth, may be used as a warm

poultice for inflammations, boils, abscesses, and rheumatic disorders. Inhaling the vapor from the soaked flowers may relieve tension and stress. Used externally, the essential oil may promote healing after burns, and helps relieve skin conditions such as eczema.

SCIENTIFIC KNOWLEDGE

Chamomile contains a volatile oil, azulene, which has two main ingredients, bisabolol and chamazule. These are proven antiseptics, which have antispasmodic and anti-inflammatory properties.

PARTS USED

The flowers and oil.

TASTE

Mild and warming.

PREPARATION

Infuse the dried flowers in hot water for a tea to calm and restore the nerves, and to help sleep. A strong infusion can be made from soaking 2 ounces of dried flowers in boiling water. This can be used as an antiseptic when cold, or even to lighten hair color. The fresh flowers can be added to bath water to aid relaxation.

CAUTIONS

No known side effects.

Chervil

Anthriscus cerefolium

Chervil, a member of the parsley family, has always been recognized as a restorative herb. Chervil tea was traditionally drunk on the Thursday before Easter to restore the system after the rigors of fasting during Lent. Its root is sometimes eaten as a vegetable.

DESCRIPTION AND HABITAT

Chervil is a small, annual herb that does not like too much sun. It has a sweet scent and delicate, feathery leaves that are aromatic when bruised. Its delicate, white flowers appear in the spring and early summer.

USES

In cooking, it is used in salads, soups, and dressings, and as an alternative to parsley. The tea is traditionally drunk to treat fluid retention, chronic catarrh, as a digestive stimulant, and to treat high blood pressure, to ease rheumatism, eczema, and jaundice. A decoction is traditionally applied to conjunctivitis (pink eye) and hemorrhoids. A cold infusion may be used as an effective skin cleanser.

SCIENTIFIC KNOWLEDGE

The leaves contain vitamin C, carotene, iron, and magnesium.

PARTS USED

The young leaves, preferably fresh.

TASTE

Mild, aniseed-like flavor.

PREPARATION

1 teaspoon to ½ cup of boiling water. Steep for a few minutes, and do not sweeten.

CAUTIONS

No known side effects.

Cinquefoil

Potentilla anserina

Also known as goose grass, silverweed, and crampweed. In the Middle Ages, it was chiefly eaten as a vegetable, and the dried leaves were used for medicinal remedies. The European variety is the creeping cinquefoil, while the American variety is the silvery cinquefoil.

DESCRIPTION AND HABITAT

Cinquefoil is a creeping perennial that grows wild in dry fields, meadows, and marshy places throughout North America and Europe. The roots put out long runners, producing a rosette of leaves that are dark green above and silver below. It has bright yellow flowers from May through September.

USES

Mixed with lemon balm, it is made into a tea to relieve cramps. Also a traditional remedy for diarrhea and as a gargle to relieve sore throats. It is used externally as an astringent to clear up skin conditions such as acne, pimples, and blackheads.

SCIENTIFIC KNOWLEDGE

Cinquefoil has a high tannin content, which is a known astringent.

PARTS USED

The root and leaves.

TASTE

Sharp and bitter, but it has no smell.

PREPARATION

To make a tea, use 1 teaspoon of the dried leaves in 1 cup of boiling water. When cold, strain and drink. Alternatively, use 2 teaspoons in hot milk as a sedative drink before bed. The root can be boiled as a vegetable, which tastes like turnip.

CAUTIONS

No known side effects.

Dandelion

Taraxacum officinale

Who, as a small child, hasn't known the delights of blowing the fuzz off a dandelion flower? This common plant, regarded as a weed by some gardeners, is a useful addition to any garden, and has long been used as a medicinal tea by the Chinese and by various Native American peoples, who gathered it in spring to use as a tonic to awaken a sluggish liver. It is also known as devil's milkwort, clock-flower, and horse lettuce. The leaves can be used fresh in salads.

DESCRIPTION AND HABITAT
Any moderate climate where grass grows. Dandelions have a bright yellow flower that turns into a soft ball of seeds—its fluffy head.

USES
Dandelion tea is a diuretic for removing excess water from the body, and it is also said to aid digestion, relieve dyspepsia, and ease liver problems. The tap root is dried and used as a coffee substitute. Fresh root and leaves are made into a decoction to soothe rheumatism and also gout.

SCIENTIFIC KNOWLEDGE
Dandelion is a proven diuretic. It is used extensively in traditional Chinese medicine for treating mastitis, breast tumors, and abscesses, as well as hepatitis and jaundice.

PARTS USED
The flowers, roots, and leaves.

TASTE
Dandelion has a mild taste.

PREPARATION
Use 2 whole fresh leaves and steep in 1 cup of hot water to make a tea. For decoction, use several whole plants, including roots, in 5 cups boiling water. Reduce to 2½ cups and allow to cool. To make a coffee substitute, the cleaned roots can be dried in a very slow oven, and then ground, and added to hot water.

CAUTIONS
Because of its diuretic qualities, some caution is advised.

Dill

Anethum graveolens

Dill grows wild in Europe, and in North and South America, where it was introduced by the early settlers. It was mentioned by Jesus in the New Testament (Matthew 23:23), and perhaps because of these biblical connotations, was often given to children to eat during the long sermons that accompanied the 19th-century religious revival movements in America, where it was known as "meetin' seed."

DESCRIPTION AND HABITAT
An annual plant that grows about 3 feet high, with blue-green leaves and yellow flowers that appear from July through September.

USES
The seeds are used in a tea for treating insomnia; fresh seeds can be chewed to relieve bad breath. A decoction is used to relieve gas and is traditionally taken by breast-feeding mothers to aid their milk production. It is also antispasmodic and diuretic, used to calm and tone the digestive system, and combat urinary infections.

SCIENTIFIC KNOWLEDGE
Dill is used extensively in the pharmaceutical trade because of its ability to ease colic. It is a principal ingredient in "gripe water" for babies.

PARTS USED
The seeds; the leaves are widely used in Scandinavian dishes containing fish and potatoes.

TASTE
Spicy and mildly bitter.

PREPARATION
To make a herbal tea, steep 2 teaspoons of seeds in 2 cups of hot water and leave to cool for 10 minutes. Traditionally used to ease wind in babies. Add honey, if liked.

CAUTIONS
Dill has always been considered especially safe for babies, but only the seeds or fresh leaves should be used—the leaves, when dried, contain a volatile oil that is quite toxic.

Fennel

Foeniculum vulgare

Originally a Mediterranean plant that now is cultivated throughout the world, fennel has been grown for thousands of years, both as a medicinal herb and as a useful herb for cooking. It was well known to both the ancient Greeks and Romans; the Greeks used it as a flavoring, while the Romans cooked it as a vegetable.

DESCRIPTION AND HABITAT

Fennel likes warmth and lots of space in which to grow. It has a finely grooved stem, and large, yellow flower-heads.

USES

The leaves can be used to flavor soups and fish dishes; the seeds chewed for fresh breath; the root is used to promote digestion as a stomachic, and the oil as a gargle for sore throats.

SCIENTIFIC KNOWLEDGE

Recent research has borne out the traditional claims that fennel increases the flow of breast milk.

PARTS USED

The seeds, roots, and leaves.

TASTE

Aromatic, spicy, a little like anise.

PREPARATION

For a herbal tea, take 1 tablespoon of fresh seeds and crush them, then add to 1 cup of hot water and leave to steep for 5 minutes. Sweeten with a little honey, and drink while still hot. For colic and to settle upset stomachs, make a decoction by boiling ½ teaspoon of fresh-crushed seeds in 1 cup of milk.

CAUTIONS

No known side effects.

Fenugreek

Trigonella foenum-graecum

Also known as Greek clover and bird's foot, this valuable plant originated in western Asia, but now grows wild around the world. It is avidly cultivated by farmers, as it is known to be a natural fertilizer and a nitrogenous aid for the soil, as well as being a good fodder plant. In traditional Chinese medicine, it has been used for centuries to treat sexual problems.

DESCRIPTION AND HABITAT
It grows about 1 to 2 feet high, with green leaves and yellow flowers that turn into long seed pods.

USES
The leaves can be used in salads, and the seeds as a spice in curries

and chutneys. The whole plant is cooked as a vegetable in curries. Freshly sprouted seeds can be eaten raw. Soaked seeds applied externally are useful as a poultice for boils and sores.

SCIENTIFIC KNOWLEDGE
Recent research has shown that the seeds contain diosgenin, which is used in the production of oral contraceptives and sex hormones. Fenugreek is now grown on a large scale by the pharmaceutical trade. In traditional Asian medicine, it has been used for centuries to treat such problems as premature ejaculation and low libido. Also used as a digestion stimulant, cough reliever, and to ease gas and diarrhea.

PARTS USED
The seeds and leaves.

TASTE
Bitter and spicy; the leaves taste of curry when young.

PREPARATION
Use 2 teaspoons of the seeds in 1 cup of cold water, then leave to stand for 6 hours. Boil for 1 minute, and drink while still hot—add honey to taste.

CAUTIONS
Should not be taken during pregnancy.

USES

The bruised leaves can be applied to insect bites. The leaves can be eaten fresh in sandwiches, as a treatment for headaches and migraines, and for relief of arthritis symptoms. It is also used to promote good sleep, ease asthma, and as a mild laxative. Cold feverfew tea makes a good mouth rinse after a tooth extraction. The dried leaves make a good insect repellent when used in pot pourri.

SCIENTIFIC KNOWLEDGE

Feverfew contains substances that appear to inhibit the natural histamines and prostaglandins that induce migraines by triggering spasms in the blood vessels of the head.

PARTS USED

The leaves.

TASTE

Quite bitter.

Feverfew

*Chrysanthemum parthenium
(Tanacetum parthenium)*

The common name of this herb suggests its traditional use by Asian and Native American peoples in easing fevers and headaches. It is one of the best-known examples of a traditional cure that has been proved by modern scientific research.

DESCRIPTION AND HABITAT

Feverfew is a strong-smelling perennial that grows up to 2 feet. Its clusters of white, daisy-like flowers appear in the summer. There are several varieties, including golden-leaved and double-flowered forms that have not been tested, but probably act in a manner similar to the common form.

PREPARATION

Take 1 heaped teaspoon per cup of boiling water. Migraine sufferers may take 1 to 2 cups a day, one tablespoon at a time.

CAUTIONS

Prolonged use of feverfew tea can result in mouth ulcers.

Ginseng

Panaxschin schin-seng

Ginseng is a small perennial native to Manchuria, now cultivated mostly in Korea. The Chinese have held ginseng in a near-religious awe for thousands of years. It is so highly prized that it now grows very rarely in the wild, and has to be especially cultivated. There is an indigenous American variety that is almost identical; it was used by Native American peoples to ease nausea and vomiting, and as an ingredient in their love potions.

DESCRIPTION AND HABITAT
Native to China; ginseng is also successfully cultivated in Korea. It is an aromatic root. The flowers are small and greenish-yellow and they are followed by clusters of small red berries which are edible.

USES
In traditional Chinese herbal medicine, ginseng is regarded as a panacea—a cure-all of sorts. It is used to treat feverish and inflammatory diseases, hemorrhage, and blood disorders, coughs, colds, and chest infections.

SCIENTIFIC KNOWLEDGE
Recent research has proven that the saponins it contains are beneficial in combating stress. Tests have proven that it is a mild stimulant, and that it can also improve concentration and endurance.

PARTS USED
The roots, collected after flowering.

TASTE
Earthy, a little like parsley.

PREPARATION
Use the root when thoroughly dry. Use ½ teaspoon ginseng to 1 cup boiling water. Take very sparingly, as the effects are strong.

CAUTIONS
Do not take during acute inflammatory disease or bronchitis, as it can worsen these. Too much ginseng can cause headaches, restlessness, and high blood pressure, especially if taken in combination with caffeine, alcohol, or spicy food.

Hawthorn

Crataegus oxyacantha

The fruits and flowers of the American hawthorn tree are famous in Native American herbal folk medicine, and they are usually associated with heart or blood-pressure remedies. In Celtic mythology, the May King and Queen were killed in the fall. The European hawthorn is often called the "May" (also called whitethorn), and is associated with themes of death, hope, and rebirth.

DESCRIPTION AND HABITAT

The hawthorn is a thorny, deciduous tree that grows up to 30 feet high and has dark green leaves with sweetly scented, white flowers, which bloom in the late spring. It also has bright red berries, which are known as haws, that appear in late fall through winter.

USES

Used for high blood pressure, angina, irregular heartbeat, spasms of the arteries, and nervous insomnia. In Asian herbal medicine, the berries are used to treat digestive disorders.

SCIENTIFIC KNOWLEDGE

Hawthorn is an adaptogen, which regulates blood pressure. It contains flavonoids and procyanidines which dilate arteries and slow the heartbeat.

PARTS USED

The berries and young buds.

TASTE

The berries are sweet and warming. The young buds have a nutty flavor.

PREPARATION

Use 2 teaspoons of dried haws (the berries) in 1 cup of hot water. Infuse for 20 minutes, then reheat.

CAUTIONS

No known side effects.

Hops

Humulus lupulus

The Romans used to eat young hop shoots as a vegetable. By the 8th century, A.D., hops were being used to make a new alcoholic beverage that became popular in Europe. This drink acquired a new name—beer—from the German. Hops are of course still used in the flavoring and production of beers.

DESCRIPTION AND HABITAT

A hardy, deciduous climber, which likes fertile, sunny sites and can grow to over 25 feet high. Hops produce male and female flowers on separate plants. The well-known yellow-green flowers are female, while the male flowers are green, smaller, and more insignificant.

USES

Hop flowers are antiseptic and said to aid digestion and ease spasms in the digestive tract. Hops are said to have a sedative effect, easing insomnia when placed in pillows as the weight of the head releases the soothing vapor of the volatile oil. The ripe, unpollinated, female flowers are used to flavor, clear, and preserve beer. The male flowers can be blanched and added to salads. The leaves can be used in soups. Adding the flowers to bath water aids relaxation. A brown dye is obtained from the leaves.

SCIENTIFIC KNOWLEDGE

Hop extracts have been found to relax muscles.

PARTS USED

The female flowers, usually dried.

TASTE

Bitter and aromatic.

PREPARATION

Use 3 teaspoons of dried flower heads to 1 cup of boiling water for a tea that helps digestion and promotes appetite, induces sleep, and alleviates nervous tension.

CAUTIONS

Avoid hops if suffering from depression, as they do have a sedative effect. Pollen from the flowers can cause dermatitis in some people.

Hyssop

Hyssopus officinalis

A very ancient herb, widely used in Mediterranean countries since biblical times (although not likely the hyssop of the Bible, which is now thought to have been confused with sweet marjoram or oregano) as a cure for rheumatism. The name comes from the Greek, where it was originally called "azob," and was regarded as a holy herb. It was used to cleanse temples because of its deodorant properties. Hyssop contains marrubin, also found in horehound, and is similarly used for lung problems, the crushed leaf can also be applied as an effective cure for the stinging itch of fire-ant bites. It is native to Europe, but now grows wild throughout North America, where it has escaped from gardens.

DESCRIPTION AND HABITAT

Hyssop grows about 2 feet high, and has pointed, dark green leaves and purply blue flowers. It is native to Europe, and now grows wild throughout America.

USES

The dried or fresh leaves can be used in cooking, and fresh leaves can be added to salads. As a tea it is taken to settle digestive and respiratory disorders, and can be used as a mouthwash.

SCIENTIFIC KNOWLEDGE

Hyssop has been shown to be beneficial in treating children for digestive and respiratory disorders. It is also a proven aid to fat digestion.

PARTS USED

Flowers and leaves, fresh or dried.

TASTE

Has a quite bitter, slightly minty taste. Use sparingly in cooking.

PREPARATION

To make a tea, use 1 teaspoon of the dried leaves and infuse in 1 cup of hot water.

CAUTIONS

No known side effects, but beware of its astringent properties.

Lavender

Lavandula officinalis

A native Mediterranean plant prized for its intense, sweet aroma, lavender has always been popular; it was added to bath water by both the Persians and the ancient Romans, and its very name (from the Latin *lavare*) means "to wash."

DESCRIPTION AND HABITAT

Lavender is a wild, native-Mediterranean shrub, with gray-green stems and leaves, and lilac-colored flowers. There are many cultivated varieties, with flower colors ranging from white to purple, and blue to lavender.

USES

Lavender is a natural sedative and antispasmodic widely used for its calming, anti-depressant qualities. It is useful for headaches, nerves, insomnia, and to ease gas. It has also been used to treat giddiness. The oil is used as a massage and bath oil, and commercially in the perfume industry. The dried herb is also used in sachets and pot pourris, and as an insect repellent.

SCIENTIFIC KNOWLEDGE

Lavender contains camphor, pinene, linabol, and terpinenol, as well as tannins, which reduce inflammation and prevent the onset of infections.

PARTS USED

Flowers and leaves. Leaves should be collected before the flowers appear.

TASTE

A sweet, aromatic flavor.

PREPARATION

To make a tea, infuse dried flowers to taste, or 1 teaspoon fresh or dried leaves in $\frac{1}{2}$ cup of boiling water.

CAUTIONS

No known side effects.

Lemon balm

Melissa officinalis

Lemon balm originated in the Middle East, but quickly spread throughout Asia and the Mediterranean countries, and it is now naturalized throughout Europe and North America. The Romans considered it sacred to Diana, goddess of the moon and the hunt, and it became an important herb across Europe. In traditional Asian herbal medicine, it was prescribed as a herb for promoting longevity. A tisane made from lemon balm that is used as a fever-sweating treatment for colds is known as Melissa Tea.

DESCRIPTION AND HABITAT

Lemon balm is a perennial that has now been naturalized in much of Europe and America. It grows about 3 feet high, and has hairy leaves and clusters of pale yellow, pink, or white flowers. The leaves smell heavily of lemons when crushed or bruised.

USES

Lemon balm was used traditionally to treat tension and depression, ease chronic, bronchial catarrh, headaches, feverish colds, and as a sedative. In cooking, the leaves can be added to salads and fruit dishes. As the plant attracts a profusion of bees, it is often planted around hives and orchards, and then rubbed on hives before introducing a new swarm. It is also used in pot pourri and herb pillows because of its aromatic, lemony scent. The leaves can also be crushed as a poultice for insect bites.

SCIENTIFIC KNOWLEDGE

The volatile oils are a natural sedative, even in very small quantities. The main oil, eugenol, is antispasmodic. Lemon balm also contains both polyphenols and tannins, which explains its effectiveness in treating viruses such as mumps and cold sores.

PARTS USED

The leaves, when fresh.

TASTE

A sweet, lemon flavor.

PREPARATION

To make a tea, infuse the fresh leaves in boiling water to taste.

CAUTIONS

No known side effects.

Lemon grass

Cymbopogon citratus

Lemon grass is relatively new to Western countries, as it originated in tropical Southeast Asia. It is also a native plant on the  Hawaiian islands, where it was used by the native Hawaiians as a kidney tonic. Its rich, lemon flavor and fragrance make it a tangy addition to hot, spicy foods, as well as a delightfully refreshing herb tea on hot days. It should now be available in almost all supermarkets, but can be obtained through mail order if not found locally.

DESCRIPTION AND HABITAT

A tender perennial grass from the tropics. It can grow over 6 feet tall, and is densely tufted, with very long, thin, pointed leaves and prominent middle veins. These leaves, when crushed, have an extremely fragrant, lemony flavor, which gives the herb its name. The flowers are greenish with a red tinge, and appear in clusters during the summer.

USES

Mainly used in Thai, Indonesian, and other Southeast Asian cuisine to flavor soups, fish, meat, and curries. It is also used in soap manufacture.

SCIENTIFIC KNOWLEDGE

It is semi-drying oil, and is therefore excellent for cleansing oily skin.

PARTS USED

Leaves, tender stalks, and oil.

TASTE

A full, lemony, spicy flavor.

PREPARATION

Make an infusion of several leaves in 1 cup of hot water.

CAUTIONS

No known side effects.

Lemon verbena

Aloysia triphylla

(Lippia citriodora)

A native of tropical America, lemon verbena is an extremely strong-scented herb that was first brought from South America to Europe by the Spanish in the 17th century. It is traditionally used throughout South America to scent finger bowls at feasts, and to give fragrance to soaps and perfumes.

DESCRIPTION AND HABITAT

Lemon verbena is a tender shrub growing up to 5 feet high. It needs a well-drained soil in a sunny position. The flowers appear in clusters at the end of the summer, and are small and pale lavender in color.

USES

In Europe, lemon verbena has been used extensively in the perfume trade, but recent evidence that it may sensitize skin to sunlight has decreased its popularity as an ingredient. It is also used in cooking, especially in stuffings, jellies, and desserts, and makes a refreshing tea that is still drunk widely in Spain and France. Lemon verbena helps combat nausea, gas, and dyspepsia, and can also ease colds and fevers.

SCIENTIFIC KNOWLEDGE

The essential oil contained in lemon verbena is known to be both antibacterial and antiseptic.

PARTS USED

The leaves and flowering tops, which should be harvested just as they begin to open.

TASTE

A strong, lemony flavor.

PREPARATION

To make a tea, infuse 1 teaspoon of dried leaves in 1 cup of boiling water for 5 minutes.

CAUTIONS

Drinking the leaf over a long period can irritate the stomach.

Lovage

Levisticum officinale

A large and beautiful plant of European origin, with a strong, celery-like taste. It was traditionally believed to be reviving—tired travelers used to put it in their shoes to refresh their feet, and enable them to continue their journeys. There is also an ancient custom of drinking a lovage "cordial," which is made from lovage, tansy, and yarrow, to relieve stomach upset. Lovage has long been used to flavor soups and stews.

DESCRIPTION AND HABITAT

A hardy perennial that grows up to 7 feet tall. It has large leaves that are aromatic when crushed. The stem is hollow, and the flowers, which are very small and greenish yellow, last from mid- through late summer. The plants take about four to five years to reach full size.

USES

In cooking, the seeds and leaves are sprinkled on soups or salads, and used to flavor cordials. The stems and stalks can be boiled or steamed as a vegetable. Medicinally, it is taken as a diuretic to reduce water retention (see *Cautions*). As a tea, it is said to help relieve the symptoms of rheumatism.

SCIENTIFIC KNOWLEDGE

Lovage helps promote the start of menstruation. Although it has a diuretic effect, it has been known to irritate the kidneys.

PARTS USED

The seeds, leaves, and roots.

TASTE

Strong and yeasty.

PREPARATION

The leaves will take a while to dry, because they are quite thick, but you can use leaves fresh or dried to make tea. Use 1 teaspoon to 1 cup of hot water.

CAUTIONS

Not to be drunk during pregnancy, or by anyone who is suffering from a kidney disorder.

Marigold/ Calendula

Calendula officinalis

One of the most versatile herbs, marigold is also known as "Marybud." The ancient Egyptians used it to delay aging, and it was regarded by the Hindus as a sacred flower. An ancient Native American remedy for wounds using marigold leaves was apparently applied to wounded soldiers on the battlefields of the American Civil War.

DESCRIPTION AND HABITAT

Marigold is an annual; it likes a moist location in full sun. It grows nearly 2 feet high, and has bright orange or yellow, daisy-like flowers. It will self-seed. The flowers should be harvested on a dry day when they are fully open.

USES

Marigold is used in skin creams for skin ulcers, as a poultice, and as a remedy for stings and burns. The leaves and flowers can be eaten in salads or used for tea. Medicinally, it is used in the treatment of ulcers and painful periods, and to bring on delayed menstruation. Traditionally, the sap is said to cure warts and corns. The oil is used in preparations for nipples cracked by breastfeeding. It can also be used as a cold infusion to make an eye salve for conjunctivitis (pink eye).

SCIENTIFIC KNOWLEDGE

It has been shown to reduce inflammation, stem bleeding, and heal damaged tissues.

PARTS USED

Flowers and young leaves.

TASTE

Fresh leaves have a salty, bitter taste.

PREPARATION

1 to 2 teaspoons of fresh or dried flowers to 1 cup of boiling water. Steep for 5 to 10 minutes. Strain and drink when cool.

CAUTIONS

Don't confuse with other related species; check with a doctor or herbal specialist if unsure. Avoid during pregnancy.

Meadowsweet

Filipendula ulmaria

Of European origin, meadowsweet was a sacred druidic plant, which is also known as queen of the meadows and bridewort. In 1838, an Italian scientist isolated salicylic acid from meadowsweet flowers, and in 1899, Bayer produced "aspirin," the name of which derives from the old Latin name for meadowsweet, *Spirea ulmaria*. Thus, meadowsweet is now known as the "herbal aspirin."

DESCRIPTION AND HABITAT

A perennial that likes rich, moist soil in at least partial sun. It grows between 2 and 3 feet high, and has cream-colored, frothy, scented flower-heads in late summer.

USES

Meadowsweet has long been used as a traditional remedy for digestive problems. It was traditionally used to flavor beer, wine, and soup, and can also be used as a dye. Flowers soaked in pure rainwater were often used as a skin freshener.

SCIENTIFIC KNOWLEDGE

Meadowsweet contains salicylates, an effective treatment for rheumatism. These can cause gastric bleeding, but it also contains tannin and mucilage, natural inhibitors of this effect.

PARTS USED

Flower heads are harvested in the fall, but young leaves may be used any time.

TASTE

A slightly almond-like flavor.

PREPARATION

Infuse 1 ounce of fresh leaves in 2½ cups of boiling water for 5 minutes. Strain before drinking.

CAUTIONS

No known side effects.

Mint

Mentha spp.

Originally a European native, the many different varieties of mint have spread around the world and been hybridized widely, all having culinary and medicinal properties. Of the various types of mint, peppermint (*Mentha piperita*) is the the most commonly used as a tea for indigestion; there are also black and curled-leaf varieties. You can make teas from other mints also, such as spearmint, apple mint, and ginger mint. Grown close to each other, they will cross-pollinate to produce just one general, unspecified sort of mint. To prevent this, pinch out the buds before they flower.

DESCRIPTION AND HABITAT

Most mints like a rich, moist soil and shade, although they will tolerate full sun. They have pink or purple flowers on spikes in late summer. The leaves are aromatic when crushed.

USES

Mint has been used traditionally as a remedy for ulcers, as a decongestant inhalant, and to treat indigestion, colic, and gas. Mint is a popular flavoring in cooking. It is used in desserts, drinks, and to accompany vegetables and meats, like lamb. If grown near roses, mint helps reduce aphid infestations.

SCIENTIFIC KNOWLEDGE

The main ingredient in the volatile oil is menthol, which is why peppermint is used in pain-relieving creams and massage oils. Menthol is an anesthetic when applied externally, and is also cooling because it increases the blood flow where it is applied.

PARTS USED

The flowering tops and leaves.

TASTE

Mints have a refreshing, distinctive taste and aroma.

PREPARATION

Pour boiling water onto a few sprigs of fresh mint to make a refreshing tea.

CAUTIONS

Never use mint oil for babies, and avoid extended use of mint oils as an inhalant.

Mullein

Verbascum thapsus

A European weed introduced to North America by settlers, mullein is also known by a wide variety of common names, including flannelleaf, Aaron's rod, and Jacob's staff. It is now commonly called yellow verbascum. Old World gypsies used to smoke the dried leaves in a pipe to cure asthma and bronchitis.

DESCRIPTION AND HABITAT

A tall, biennial plant. The yellow flowers grow in tall spikes throughout the summer. The leaves are thick and light-green, with a soft, hairy appearance. It is known as "white" mullein in the U.S., but it is closely related to the "black" mullein that grows throughout Europe. The two plants are the same for teas and medicinal purposes.

USES

The flower tea may help relieve pain and induce sleep. A handful of flowers in hot water makes a vapor that relieves nasal congestion, bronchial catarrh, and whooping cough.

SCIENTIFIC KNOWLEDGE

Its two principal active ingredients—saponin and mucilage—make mullein a soothing expectorant for treating hoarseness, sore throats, coughs, asthma, and bronchitis.

PARTS USED

The flowers and leaves.

TASTE

Flowers are sweeter than the leaves.

PREPARATION

The leaves boiled or steeped in vinegar and hot water can be used externally for relieving inflammation and painful skin conditions. A poultice of leaves is said to be most helpful for difficult sores and wounds.

CAUTIONS

If the leaves are used as an infusion, the liquid should be strained through cheesecloth before being drunk.

Nettle

Urtica dioica

Stinging nettle is a European native originating in the Mediterranean countries. The Latin name *urtica* comes from "urere," meaning "to burn," on account of its stinging hairs. Nettles are grown commercially and processed to extract chlorophyll, which is used to color foods and medicines.

DESCRIPTION AND HABITAT

Nettle grows wild on any soil. It is a perennial growing up to 4 feet high. The pointed leaves are toothed, and the flowers insignificant.

USES

Nettle tea is used by herbalists to treat gout and arthritis, because it is thought to stimulate the excretion of uric acid. In addition, nettles have been used to reduce bleeding, ease excessive menstruation, lower blood sugar, and encourage the flow of breast milk. Nettles are an ingredient of many shampoos and hair treatments, as they make the hair glossy and reduce dandruff. The leaves can be cooked in soups and stews, and also eaten as a vegetable.

SCIENTIFIC KNOWLEDGE

Nettles contain vitamins A and C, and minerals including iron.

PARTS USED

All above-ground parts of the young plants are used.

TASTE

The leaves are quite bland.

PREPARATION

Wear gloves to collect nettles. The sting is removed by boiling or drying. For a tea, use 2 to 3 tablespoons of leaves steeped in hot water for 10 minutes.

CAUTIONS

Only use young plants, as older plants can be toxic eaten raw and may cause kidney damage.

Oregano

Origanum vulgare

Oregano, also known as wild marjoram, is a native of Greece, where it grows on the hillsides. Its name comes from the Greek for "joy-of-the-mountain." The ancient Greeks believed that it was an antidote to poison; Aristotle claimed that any tortoise that swallowed a snake would eat oregano straight afterwards for this reason. Its use spread across Europe during medieval times, where it was valued for "nosegays" and for strewing, because of its spicy smell; it was also believed to ward off the plague.

DESCRIPTION AND HABITAT

A hardy perennial that grows 2 feet high in frequent sunshine. The stems are reddish with dark, pointed leaves. The small, whitish pink flowers grow in clusters at the tips of the stems.

USES

Oregano is used to treat wind, stomach upsets, and indigestion. It stimulates the uterus, and eases painful menstruation. It increases sweating and is also a mild expectorant. It is a popular culinary herb in many Mediterranean dishes, such as pizza. The oil is

used commercially to flavor food, and is also used in cosmetics and men's perfumes, and for killing lice. A few leaves under the hot tap make a relaxing bath. Use a strong infusion as a hair conditioner. Chewing the leaves will give temporary relief from toothache. The tea also helps to ease sea-sickness.

SCIENTIFIC KNOWLEDGE

The leaves contain thymol, which is a strong antiseptic.

PARTS USED

The leaves and flowering tops.

TASTE

Sweet and peppery.

PREPARATION

Use 1 teaspoon of dried herb in 1 cup of hot water. Steep for 5 minutes.

CAUTIONS

Avoid during pregnancy.

Parsley

Petroselinum crispum

A native Mediterranean plant, the Romans seem to have been the first to use it as a food plant. They also used garlands of parsley to discourage drunkenness and to mask bad breath. It is still chewed to reduce the smell of garlic. Italian parsley is a variety of flat-leafed parsley native to Asian and Mediterranean countries; this is used for cooking as well as for treating urinary tract infections.

DESCRIPTION AND HABITAT

Parsley is a biennial, and prefers a rich soil in sun or semi-shade. It grows about 2 feet high, and has dark green, curled leaves. It has small, greenish yellow flowers in the summer.

USES

Parsley is a strong diuretic that is often used to treat kidney problems. It is said to strengthen the muscles of the uterus, and improve the milk flow, and is used as a garnish in cooking. Seeds and leaves can be steeped in boiling water to make a golden hair rinse. Parsley can also be used as a dye.

SCIENTIFIC KNOWLEDGE

Parsley contains a flavonoid, which reduces allergic responses.

PARTS USED

The leaves, seeds, and stems.

TASTE

A sweet, tangy flavor.

PREPARATION

Dried parsley leaves retain more flavor the faster they are dried. To make a tea, put 1 tablespoon of leaves, fresh or dried, in 1 cup of boiling water, and steep for 20 minutes before drinking.

CAUTIONS

Avoid in medicinal doses during pregnancy. Can be toxic in very large quantities. Never eat the seeds because they are poisonous.

Pennyroyal

Mentha pulegium

Native to Europe and Western Asia, pennyroyal is also known as "pudding grass" and "lurk-in-the-dark." The Latin name comes from *pulex*, meaning "a flea," because it is an effective insect repellant. The oil is used in detergents. Pennyroyal was traditionally used by sailors to purify drinking water.

DESCRIPTION AND HABITAT

A hardy perennial with smooth, bright green leaves and a peppermint scent. There are two varieties—a creeping variety and an upright variety. They both spread by rooting stems, and have pale flowers.

USES

Pennyroyal in hot infusions promotes sweating, brings on menstruation, aids digestion, and is used to treat cold and flu symptoms. The tea, taken with a little honey, is also used to ease asthma. It may also be applied externally as a wash for rashes and skin eruptions. The leaves are often added to pot pourri. A little of the dried leaves steeped in vinegar makes an excellent "smelling salt" for reviving faints.

SCIENTIFIC KNOWLEDGE

The volatile oil can be highly poisonous. It brings on menstruation, and a number of women have died taking it to bring on abortion.

PARTS USED

The leaves and flowering tops.

TASTE

Minty and somewhat bitter.

PREPARATION

One tablespoon of dried leaves in 1 cup of boiling water. Drink 1 to 2 cups per day.

CAUTIONS

Never take if pregnant, or if pregnancy is suspected.

Plantain

Plantago major

Plantain is also known as ribwort and snakeweed. It is a European native, now naturalized everywhere. It was traditionally believed to increase fertility, probably because of the phallic-shaped flower spikes— but there doesn't seem to be any scientific evidence to support this belief. The edible leaves are also used as a poultice to reduce allergic reactions and skin inflammation.

DESCRIPTION AND HABITAT

Plantain is a perennial, which grows about 18 inches tall, and has broad, oval leaves with long spikes of greenish white flowers that bloom throughout the summer.

USES

Plantain is an expectorant, an astringent, a diuretic, a demulcent (soothes irritation), and is antibacterial. The crushed leaves can be applied to varicose veins and hemorrhoids. Plantain reduces bleeding, and decoctions can also be applied directly to the skin to treat ringworm. Chewing the root eases toothache, and the seeds, which contain up to 30 percent mucilage, a gluey mixture of carbohydrates, swell in the digestive tract, acting as a natural laxative.

SCIENTIFIC KNOWLEDGE

Plantain contains silica which is good for use as a natural laxative. It also contains tannin which is effective against bacterial infections. This explains why it is effective in stopping bleeding and reducing hemorrhoids and varicose veins.

PARTS USED

The leaves and roots.

TASTE

Rather astringent.

PREPARATION

The leaves can be dried normally and stored in glass jars. Use 1 teaspoon infused in ½ cup of boiling water.

CAUTIONS

No known side effects.

Raspberry leaf

Rubus stigosus (Rubus idaeus)

The North American wild raspberry (*Rubus stigosus*) is generally grown for its fruit; the European red raspberry (*R. idaeus*) has the same properties. Raspberry-leaf tea is said to relieve muscular spasms during labor; it is also recommended in Native American lore to relieve menstrual cramps. It was first mentioned as a medicinal herb in ancient Greece as long ago as 400 B.C.

DESCRIPTION AND HABITAT

The raspberry is a perennial, shrubby plant that has few thorns. It has dark green leaves that are silvery underneath, and small clusters of white flowers in the spring. It produces dark red fruit in its second year.

USES

The fruit is widely used in cooking, and a cold infusion of the leaves is used as a mouthwash or gargle for mouth ulcers, sores, and tonsilitis.

SCIENTIFIC KNOWLEDGE

The leaves contain tannins and flavonoids; recent research has also isolated a substance called fragarine, which seems to be responsible for this plant's ability to relax the uterus.

PARTS USED

The leaves and fruit.

TASTE

The leaves can be quite strong and unpleasant, and should be sweetened with honey if taken as a tea. The fruit is sweet and sharp.

PREPARATION

Use 1 to 2 tablespoons steeped in ½ cup of boiling water. Take 1 cup per day.

CAUTIONS

No known side effects.

Rosehip

Rosa spp.

All roses have a variety of "herbal" uses—the petals are edible, and are used to make pot pourris, perfumes, and other scented products; the essential oil is used in aromatherapy; and the "hips" (the buds remaining after the flower has fallen) are a rich source of vitamin C. Roses were originally cultivated in Persia, to make rose wine; their use spread across the Middle East, Asia, and Europe. The Chinese made a tea from the large-hip rose (now naturalized in the United States) for promoting blood circulation; there are other Chinese-originated varieties now naturalized throughout America, such as the Cherokee rose (*Rosa laevigata*), and the sweet briar rose (*R. rugosa*). The so-called "mad-dog rose" (from the medieval belief that it could cure the bite of a mad dog), is often used in making tea, because of the large quantities of vitamin C in the hips.

DESCRIPTION AND HABITAT
A hardy, rambling, or upright shrub with elliptical leaves; the stems are usually covered in thorns. The flowers are usually pink, and are single on the dog rose, with five petals. Other roses have white, red, purple, or yellow flowers. Most roses flower in the summer, and are known for their fragrance.

USES
Rosehips are a good source of vitamin C (especially the dog rose); and are used in cooking to give a sharp flavor to desserts and syrups. Rosewater is the principal flavoring in Turkish Delight, and is used as a perfume, and an antiseptic skin tonic. Rosewater may also soothe conjunctivitis (pink eye) if splashed on the eyes.

SCIENTIFIC KNOWLEDGE
The value of rosehips as a source of vitamin C was first recognized during the Second World War, when they were collected in large numbers from hedges and made into a syrup.

PARTS USED
The hips and leaves can both be used for teas.

TASTE
Sweet and tangy.

PREPARATION
The hips should be collected, cut in half, and dried quickly with an electric heater, or in the oven, to keep their color. To make a tea, boil a handful of rosehips in water for 5 minutes. Strain before drinking.

CAUTIONS
No known side effects.

Rosemary
Rosmarinus officinalis

An ancient, native Mediterranean plant, rosemary was believed to improve the memory and its scent was thought to be purifying. Rosemary can be grown anywhere and used for abundant purposes.

DESCRIPTION AND HABITAT
An evergreen, woody perennial. Rosemary likes a well-drained soil, not too acidic, and prefers full sunshine. Some varieties can grow up to 6 feet tall and it carries its blue flowers through the winter in more moderate climates. There are numerous cultivated varieties.

USES
Traditionally taken as a tea for headaches, poor digestion, and bad circulation, the essential oil is also antibacterial and antifungal. Rosemary is said to reduce gas, stimulate digestion, and ease painful periods. It is used to flavor meat and fish dishes, and is often an ingredient in shampoos and hair treatments for dandruff.

SCIENTIFIC KNOWLEDGE
Rosemary contains a flavonoid called diosmin, which improves the circulation and strengthens blood vessels that are damaged or fragile.

PARTS USED
The leaves.

TASTE
Strong, pungent, and pleasant.

PREPARATION
To make a tea, use 1 teaspoon in 1 cup of hot water.

CAUTIONS
Do not take for more than a few days at a time. Avoid during pregnancy.

Sage
Salvia officinalis

The classic species of sage originates in Spain and the Balkan countries; its Latin name comes from *salvare*, which means "to save," because of the plant's well-known healing properties. Native American peoples burned an indigenous type of sage in their ceremonies, and they believed that it should never be bought or sold, because this would ruin the spirituality of the herb. The Chinese, however, were so intrigued by this herb that they used to trade their best tea for sage with the Dutch, giving three times the quantity of tea to sage.

DESCRIPTION AND HABITAT
Sage grows in well-drained, non-acidic soil in sunny positions, and is an evergreen, perennial shrub. It can grow up to 2 feet high and in summer has purple, blue, or pink flowers. The leaves are soft, gray-green and aromatic when crushed. Purple, golden, and variegated-leaf varieties are grown.

USES
Sage tea with cider vinegar is used as a mouthwash for sore throats, laryngitis, and tonsilitis. The tea is used for mouth ulcers and to treat heavy, painful periods. It is also used in cooking.

SCIENTIFIC KNOWLEDGE
Sage is a proven remedy for colds; it contains phenolic acid, which is antibacterial, and thujone, which is a strong antiseptic. Because it contains estrogenic substances, sage is used to treat menopausal symptoms.

PARTS USED
The young leaves.

TASTE
Warm and pungent, with a slight hint of camphor.

PREPARATION
Careful drying is important. Use fresh leaf sprigs in boiling water to make a simple tea.

CAUTIONS
Sage tea should not be taken for more than a few weeks at a time.

Skullcap

Scutellaria baicalensis

A native North American and Asian plant, skullcap is also known as the helmet flower because of the shape of its flowers, and as mad-dogweed, because it was thought to cure rabies and epilepsy. It was used by the Cherokee people to promote menstruation. It was first mentioned around 200 A.D. in Chinese herbal medicine, and is used to treat all manner of kidney disorders.

DESCRIPTION AND HABITAT
A perennial that likes a moist soil in full or partial sun. It grows 2 feet high, and has small, blue flowers in the summer at the ends of the leaf stems.

USES
The powdered herb can be infused as a tea, and taken as a remedy for premenstrual tension, rheumatism, and severe hiccups. It is used to treat nervous disorders, migraines, depression, insomnia, and restlessness, and to ease withdrawal from tranquilizers and barbiturates.

SCIENTIFIC KNOWLEDGE
Skullcap contains flavonoid glycosides, plant chemicals that act as diuretics and antispasmodics.

PARTS USED
The leaves.

TASTE
Very bitter; sweeten with honey if using as a tea.

PREPARATION
Use 1 teaspoon of leaves, fresh or dried, steeped in 1 cup of boiling water for 30 minutes.

CAUTIONS
Avoid during pregnancy. Too much skullcap can cause dizziness and twitching. Commercially sold skullcap may actually be wood sage (*Teucrium scorodonia*), and not real skullcap. To be certain, your best bet is to grow it yourself.

St. John's wort

Hypericum perforatum

This European native plant is reputed to flower on the eve of St. John's day (June 24th), hence its name. It has been in use and recognized as a powerful medicinal herb for several thousand years. Traditionally, the plant was always picked at the summer solstice and used as a charm to protect against evil; it was also used medicinally, with an infusion from the flower oils made into a pain-reducing, sedative tea to treat various anemic, rheumatic, headache, and nervous conditions. It is now considered unsafe by some.

DESCRIPTION AND HABITAT
St. John's wort thrives in sunny situations, growing up to 3 feet high, and has pale green leaves with bright yellow flowers.

USES
It makes a pleasant tea, and is used for treating depression as well as dispelling gloom and raising the spirits. It can be used as a lotion to help wound healing, and may help reduce muscle tension.

SCIENTIFIC KNOWLEDGE
Clinical trials have proved its effectiveness in treating depression, and it is widely used for this. It is now being tested for its potential development as an antiviral drug.

PARTS USED
The flowering tops, which are picked as soon as the flowers open during the summer.

TASTE
Mildly bitter and astringent.

PREPARATION
Make an infusion using 1 teaspoon per cup.

CAUTIONS
There are no known side effects, though in certain cases, it can cause digestive upsets.

Strawberry

Fragaria vesca

The strawberry, which can easily be grown in your garden, is nearly everyone's favorite berry fruit. Wild strawberries grow in the cool, hidden woodlands of Europe and North America, and have thus often been associated with fairy folk. The fruit is used in cooking, baking, and eaten fresh, while the leaves, which are rich in vitamin C, are often used to make teas for treating anemia, nervous disorders, diarrhea, gastro-intestinal and urinary tract disorders, and as a tonic for kidneys.

DESCRIPTION AND HABITAT

A hardy perennial that grows 10 inches high. It is a natural woodland plant, that likes a moist, shady, well-drained site. The fruit is smaller than cultivated varieties, but is sweeter and tastier.

USES

The tea is used as a treatment for anemia, diarrhea, and other digestive disorders, and as a diuretic and tonic for the kidneys. The root can also be used as a tonic and diuretic. Eaten fresh, the fruit provides a mild-laxative action. The juice has been used as a natural teeth cleaner. Crushed strawberries rubbed onto the face are said to relieve the stinging of sunburn. The bruised leaves can be added to meat stews and stocks to add flavor. A tea made from the leaf makes a good astringent toner for oily skin.

SCIENTIFIC KNOWLEDGE

Strawberry leaf is rich in vitamin C, and the leaf and fruit contain iron, which is why it can be helpful in the treatment of anemia.

PARTS USED

The root, leaves, and fruit. The leaves should be dried thoroughly, because the process of wilting produces a toxin that disappears once the drying process is complete.

TASTE

Sweet, pleasant.

PREPARATION

Dry the leaves thoroughly and infuse 1 teaspoon to 1 cup of boiling water.

CAUTIONS

No known side effects.

Thyme

Thymus vulgaris

Wild thyme (*Thymus serpyllum*) has similar properties to garden thyme (*T. vulgaris*). A Mediterranean native, thyme was traditionally believed to bestow courage; the name comes from the Greek *thymon*, which means courage, and Roman soldiers added thyme to their bathing waters. The American variety, creeping thyme (*T. praecox*), can withstand heat and humidity better than its European relative, and can be used in the same ways for cooking, aromatherapy, and medicinal purposes.

DESCRIPTION AND HABITAT

Thyme prefers a light, well-drained soil in a sunny location. Wild thyme is an evergreen shrub growing up to 15 inches, but other varieties may be considerably smaller. The leaves are small and aromatic, and it has pale pink or purple flowers.

USES

Thyme is widely used in cooking as an aromatic herb, especially in meat and poultry dishes, and in stuffings. Medicinally, it is used to treat sore throats, colds, coughs, and flu symptoms. Thyme infused in the bath is used to ease rheumatism, and the volatile oil from the plant is used in ointments and massage oils. It is also used externally to treat shingles.

SCIENTIFIC KNOWLEDGE

One of the main components of the oil is thymol, which is antibacterial and antifungal. It is used to treat worms, and is a natural pesticide.

PARTS USED

The leaves and stalks.

TASTE

Strong, slightly sharp flavor.

PREPARATION

The sprigs should be laid out in the dark to dry. Store in dark jars. To make thyme tea, infuse 2 teaspoons of thyme in 1 cup of hot water.

CAUTIONS

Do not take if pregnant. The volatile oil is quite toxic, and should only be used externally in small quantities.

Valerian

Valeriana officinalis

Valerian is also known as garden heliotrope, all-heal, and setwall. It is a native of Europe and Western Asia. Valerian comes from the Latin *valere*, meaning to be healthy. The fresh root smells of old leather. Its smell is reputed to attract cats, rats, and mice.

DESCRIPTION AND HABITAT

Valerian is a hardy perennial that grows from 2 to 5 feet high. There are several valerians; this wild variety can be identified by the deep grooves down its stem. It has narrow, dark green leaflets, and tiny, pale pink flowers.

USES

Tincture of valerian is thought to cure dandruff, but it is primarily used to treat nervous tension, headaches, and insomnia. It has antispasmodic properties and can be used to treat stomach cramps, irritable bowel syndrome, nervous dyspepsia, and menstrual cramps.

SCIENTIFIC KNOWLEDGE

It is the valepotriates in valerian that account for its sedative effect.

PARTS USED

The roots, which should be dried in the dark before use.

TASTE

Mild, not particularly pleasant; can be sweetened with a little honey.

PREPARATION

Put 1 teaspoon of dried root in 1 cup of cold water. Leave to steep at least overnight, then strain, and drink cold.

CAUTIONS

Large doses or continuous use over long periods is not advisable. Don't take for more than 2 to 3 weeks without a few days' break.

Vervain

Verbena officinalis

Vervain, which originated in the Middle East and spread throughout Europe and Asia, was a sacred herb in many ancient cultures—the Egyptians believed it sprang from the tears of Isis; the ancient Greeks and Romans consecrated it to Venus; the Anglo-Saxons considered it to be a powerful protector and salve against disease; and both the druids and the Persian magi used it in their rites of prophecy and visions. The Chinese have also long valued it as a healing herb, giving it names such as dragon-teeth grass and iron vervain to imply its potency.

DESCRIPTION AND HABITAT

Vervain is a hardy perennial that grows up to 3 feet when planted in well-drained soil and kept in sun or light shade. It has narrow, lobed leaves like stretched oak leaves, and small, pale pink flowers.

USES

The infused leaves are used in a mouthwash for sore throats, and a cold compress for sore, tired eyes. Vervain is a herbal treatment for liver and gall bladder diseases, and relieves the symptoms of nervous exhaustion, depression, headaches, and migraines.

SCIENTIFIC KNOWLEDGE

Vervain contains glycosides, which increase the flow of breast milk, and brings on menstruation.

PARTS USED

Leaves and stalks.

TASTE

Slightly bitter, sweeten with honey.

PREPARATION

Put 1 teaspoon of fresh or dried herb in 1 cup of boiling water. Steep for 5 minutes.

CAUTIONS

Avoid during pregnancy. Do not confuse with lemon verbena.

Yarrow

Achillea millefolium

Yarrow is a native of Europe and Western Asia, also known as nose bleed and thousand leaf. The Chinese use yarrow leaf in traditional herbal medicine. The *I Ching*, or Book of Changes, is an ancient system of divination using yarrow stalks. Yarrow's wound-healing properties were famous beyond China; its Latin name derives from the legend that Achilles apparently used yarrow to treat his soldiers' wounds.

DESCRIPTION AND HABITAT

A hardy perennial, yarrow grows from 1 to 3 feet high in sun or light shade. The leaves are narrow, aromatic, and feathery. It has white or pink flowers.

USES

A traditional treatment for rheumatism. Medicinally, also used to treat colds and flu, internal and external bleeds, hemorrhoids, to stimulate the digestive system, and heal wounds. Often used in skin cleansers for its toning properties.

SCIENTIFIC KNOWLEDGE

Yarrow contains tannins, which is why it heals wounds. It also contains flavonoids, which dilate peripheral arteries and encourage better blood flow to the skin, which both cools any fever and lowers blood pressure, as well as eliminating blood clots.

PARTS USED

All above-ground parts. The infused leaves make a good skin freshener.

TASTE

Slightly bitter, peppery, pleasant.

PREPARATION

Use 1 teaspoon of fresh or dried herb to 1 cup of boiling water.

CAUTIONS

The leaves, if used topically for too long, can make the skin very sensitive to light and sunburn.

Great combinations

While single varieties of herbal teas such as chamomile and mint are popular as bedtime and after-meal drinks, mixing and matching herbs can greatly increase enjoyment and health benefits. We offer a mere selection of the variety of combinations that you could try, which should prove a delicious and exciting taster of what can be done by mixing herbs and adding other ingredients such as fruit (or alcohol!)

Try our classic combinations of herbs, the hot and spicy mixtures suggested in Winter Warmers, or the ice-cold and refreshing ideas given in Summer Coolers.

Children too can enjoy exciting combinations, and they make a much healthier alternative to the drinks they are normally attracted to. So get mixing! Any combination can be tried, but if in doubt it is advisable to take professional advice.

Fresh herbs have been used in the recipes where the flavor of these is superior, and if they are likely to be readily available. However, dried herbs may be substituted throughout. Organic or unwaxed citrus fruit is recommended, especially where grated peel is used to flavor or decorate drinks. For general instructions on making herb teas, see pages 10–11.

Chamomile, *fennel, and sage tea*

Fennel and sage bring an extra flavor dimension to the soothing and calming qualities of chamomile, making this tea a good digestive aid.

Serves 4

1 tsp dried chamomile
1 Tbsp dried fennel
2 chopped, fresh sage leaves or
  ½ tsp dried sage
2½ cups freshly boiled water

Put the herbs in a tea pot or your chosen container for making herbal teas. Pour the water over them and leave to brew for 3 minutes, or longer, if you prefer a stronger, more pungent flavor.

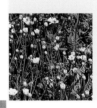

Chamomile *and mint tea*

Combining the aromatic taste of mint with the softer features of chamomile produces an ideal, after-meal herbal tea.

Serves 4

4 tsp dried chamomile
3 to 4 sprigs fresh mint, or
  1 tsp dried mint
2½ cups freshly boiled water

Put the herbs in a tea pot or your chosen container for making herbal teas. Pour the water over them and leave to brew for 4 minutes, or longer, if you prefer a stronger, more pungent flavor.

Chamomile *tea and honey*

A popular bedtime or soothing drink for colds and sore throats. Acacia honey is clear, with a distinctive, fragrant flavor that delicately enhances the chamomile. Acacia has the benefit of not crystalizing into a set honey, which other clear honeys do over time. However, if you prefer the flavor of another variety of honey, substitute it for acacia.

Serves 1

1 tsp dried chamomile
½ cup freshly boiled water
Acacia honey to taste

Put the chamomile in an individual tea pot or your chosen container for making herbal teas. Pour the water over it and leave to brew for 3 to 5 minutes. Pour the tea through a tea strainer, and add the honey to taste when serving.

Marigold, *lemon verbena, and rosehip tea*

A golden, flavorful tea with a tangy taste, excellent for waking up the tastebuds in the morning!

Serves 4

3 tsp dried marigold flowers and/or leaves
2 tsp dried lemon verbena
2 tsp dried, chopped rosehips or rosehip granules (crushed rosehips)
2½ cups boiling water

Put the herbs in a tea pot or your chosen container for making herbal teas. Pour over the water and leave to brew for 4 minutes; any longer will result in a slightly bitter flavor.

Blackberry *and apple tea*

A fresh-tasting, fruity tea that combines the tangy taste of blackberry leaves with a sweet, fresh, apple flavor.

Serves 3

1 thinly sliced dessert apple, do not peel or core
1¾ cups freshly boiled water
2 tsp blackberry leaves

Put the apple slices in a saucepan with the water and bring to a boil. Lower the heat, stir in the blackberry leaves, and simmer for five minutes. Remove from the heat, mash the apple with a fork, and strain the tea through a sieve into a warmed tea pot. Pour at once through a tea strainer.

Blackberry *and nettle tea*

This mildly tangy green tea has a soft, classic herbal-tea flavor. Try out both versions using fresh and dried nettles to find your favorite. Do not forget to wear protective gloves if using fresh nettles.

Serves 4

2 tsp dried blackberry leaves
3 Tbsp fresh nettle leaves or 3 tsp dried nettles
2½ cups freshly boiled water

Put the herbs in a tea pot or your chosen container for making herbal teas. Pour over the water and leave to brew for 4 minutes, or longer if you prefer a more pungent flavor. Pour through a tea strainer.

Mullein, *lemon grass, and mint tea*

Lemon grass and mint are complementary in this extremely refreshing tea. The light, lemon-mint flavor makes it ideal for serving with Asian food. Dried mullein is used to prevent irritation from hairs on the leaves of fresh mullein.

Serves 4

2 tsp dried mullein
3 tsp dried lemon grass
4 sprigs fresh mint
2½ cups freshly boiled water

Put the herbs in a tea pot or your chosen container for making herbal teas. Pour over the water and leave to brew for 5 minutes. Then pour through a tea strainer and serve.

Rosehip, *lemon verbena, fennel, mint, and raspberry tea*

A marvelously rich herbal tea in which the herbs are blended to a soothing, amber nectar.

Serves 6

2 tsp dried, chopped rosehips or
rosehip granules (crushed
rosehips)
1 Tbsp dried lemon verbena
2 tsp dried fennel
2 sprigs fresh mint or ½ teaspoon
dried mint
2 tsp dried raspberry leaves
4 cups freshly boiled water

Put the herbs in a tea pot or your chosen container for making herbal teas. Pour over the water and leave to brew for 4 minutes. Pour through a tea strainer.

Black currant, *ginseng, and vanilla tea*

This delicious, fruity tea can be made with either fresh or frozen black currants.

Serves 3

1 cup black currants, fresh or frozen, or 2 Tbsp black currant cordial
¼ cup sugar
1¼ cups freshly boiled water
½ tsp dried ginseng root
½ vanilla bean, split
2 Tbsp black currant cordial

Wash the fruit and put in a saucepan with the sugar, and enough water to cover the base of the pan to prevent burning. Simmer over a low heat to extract the juice from the black currants. Strain into a cup and put to one side. Put the ginseng and vanilla in a tea pot or your chosen container for making herbal teas. Pour over the water and steep for 3 minutes. Stir in the black currant cordial and let stand for 2 minutes. Pour through a tea strainer. Rinse the vanilla bean and cut into small pieces, adding one piece to each cup.

Do not be concerned about small, black specks in the tea; these are from the vanilla bean.

Winter Warmers

When the nights draw in, what better way to keep the chills at bay than to sip one of these Winter Warmer herbal drinks. Each recipe has a bite to it, whether spicy or alcoholic, and all of them are served piping hot, except for Lemon-balm claret cup which, despite being served cold, delivers a warming kick all of its own.

Chamomile *and spiced apple*

Serves 6

2 oz dried chamomile
2 cloves
3 green cardamoms
½ apple, unpeeled and sliced
1 cinnamon stick
Honey, light brown sugar, or maple syrup to serve

Put all the ingredients in a saucepan and bring a boil. Lower the heat, stir, and simmer for 5 minutes. Remove from the heat and pour into a cold container. Let stand for 5 minutes. Strain and pour into a jug or warmed tea pot to serve. The apple slices and cinnamon may be rinsed and added to the jug when the tea is served. Sweeten to taste with honey, light brown sugar, or maple syrup.

Lemon, *ginger, and valerian tea*

Serves 4

1 teaspoon dried valerian
1 teaspoon freshly grated,
   peeled ginger root
2½ cups freshly boiled water
Juice of ½ lemon
2–3 teaspoons clear honey

Put the valerian and ginger in a tea pot or your chosen container for making herbal teas. Pour over the water and leave to brew for 3 minutes. Stir in the lemon juice and honey. Pour through a tea strainer.

Athole *brose*

A warming Scottish drink for adults. A brose is a traditional Scottish dish made by pouring hot water onto oatmeal.

Serves 6

1 apple, peeled, cored, and
   thinly sliced
¼ cup medium oatmeal
1 oz dried mullein
3½ cups boiling water
1 measure (1½ Tbsp) whisky
concentrated apple juice or
   honey to sweeten

Put the dry ingredients in a large container and pour over the water. Let stand until cool enough to drink. Strain and pour into cups, adjust strength by adding more hot water. Add the whisky and sweeten to taste. It is also good cold, so alternatively, refrigerate before serving.

Lemon-Balm *claret cup*

Although this is a chilled drink, it has a warming effect. The recipe is from the head of the Royal Kitchen in the early reign of Queen Victoria of England, and is part of a collection of recipes in Flowers as Food by Florence White, published by Jonathan Cape, London, England, 1934. Florence White, formerly a cook in country houses, traveled throughout England in the 1930s taking a scholarly approach to collecting traditional English recipes. Substitute red wine of your choice for the recommended Bordeaux red wine. The drink is also good without the Cognac (brandy). Use brown sugar instead of bruised candy-sugar.

Serves 10

1 bottle claret
1 small bunch of lemon balm
1 small bunch of borage
1 orange, sliced
½ cucumber, sliced thick
1 liqueur glass of Cognac
1 oz bruised-sugar candy
1½ cups chilled soda water

Put all ingredients except the soda water in a jug over ice for 1 hour, then stir well, strain, and add the chilled soda water.

Cider *cup*

Serves 12

½ oz lemon verbena
½ oz borage
½ cup sugar
1¼ cups freshly boiled water
1 orange, thinly sliced
Juice of ½ lemon
Juice and pared rind of ½ orange

4½ cups alcoholic or plain apple cider

Put the herbs in a basin with the sugar and pour over the boiling water. Leave to steep for 10 minutes. Strain and cool. Just before serving, put ice cubes in a serving jug, add the orange slices, and pour over the lemon and orange juice, and orange rind. Pour over the cider and stir well. Serve at once.

Summer Coolers

Iced herbal teas make a refreshing summer drink. If using teabags, make double-strength tea (chilling reduces the flavor), cool, and transfer to the fridge for about an hour to chill. Pour over ice to serve.

Apple, *mint, and cranberry cooler*

Serves 4

4 Tbsp dried cranberries
2 sprigs fresh mint
1 apple, peeled and sliced
1¾ cups freshly boiled water

Put all the ingredients in a large tea pot, jug, or other container, and pour over the water. Let stand for 1 hour. Strain and chill before pouring over ice.

With Alcohol 1½ Tbsp cup grenadine and either 1 measure (1½ Tbsp) gin or vodka per glass.

Tomato *and parsley sling*

Serves 4

**2½ cups tomato (or mixed
    vegetable) juice**
1 small bunch parsley
**Worcestershire (or soy) sauce
    to taste**

Put the tomato or vegetable juice
and parsley in a blender or food
processor and blend. Pour over ice,
and season with Worcestershire or
soy sauce to taste.

With Alcohol Add 1 measure (1½
Tbsp) vodka per glass.

Nettle-Ginger *beer*

*This traditional, still ginger beer is also excellent mixed half-and-half either
with lemonade or soda water.*

Makes approximately 10 glasses

**4 oz fresh ginger root, roughly
    chopped**
4 cups water
½ cup superfine sugar
2 Tbsp dried nettles
2 tsp grated orange rind
1 cinnamon stick

Put the roughly chopped ginger root
and 1 cup water in a blender or food
processor and blend. Dissolve the
sugar in 1 cup of the water in a pan
or microwave oven. Put all the
ingredients in a jug or other
container with a lid. Stir well and let
stand in a cool place for 24 hours.
Strain, put in the fridge to chill for
about 1 hour, pour over ice to serve.

With Alcohol Add 1 measure (1½
Tbsp) whisky or bourbon per glass.

Pink *mint-julep*

Serves 5

**1 Tbsp light-brown sugar (or
  white sugar
  for a more delicate color)**
2½ cups boiling water
4 sprigs of mint
**1 cup black currants, fresh or
  frozen**

Dissolve the sugar in the water. Add
the mint and black currants and mash
the black currants partially with a fork.
Let stand until cool. Transfer to the
fridge and serve over ice.

With Alcohol Add 1 measure (1½
Tbsp) rum per glass. White rum (e.g.
Bacardi) produces a more delicately
flavored and colored drink, while
dark rum produces a richer, sweeter,
darker-colored drink.

Lemonade *Mimosa*

*Mimosa is usually made by mixing champagne or other sparkling white wine
with orange juice. Instead of orange juice, use the Old-Fashioned Lemonade
in the Children's Drinks section as a mixer with sparkling wine.*

Herbs for Health

Colds and Flu

There is no cure for a cold, but the symptoms can be somewhat alleviated. The traditional remedy of honey and hot lemon is invaluable. You can also add a few fresh leaves of sage to reduce fever or, if you feel cold, then a warming tea can be made with fresh ginger root, fennel, and honey. For a blocked nose, try a steam inhalation of chamomile flowers in hot water—or eucalyptus leaves (if you can't get fresh leaves, substitute eucalyptus oil).

Cystitis

During an attach of cystitis, drinking yarrow tea, a standard infusion, three times a day is advised by herbalists.

Digestive Disorders

There are some common causes that may be easy to identify, such as poor appetite following an illness, or an upset stomach due to stress. In the case of home diagnosis, only the simplest and most obvious conditions should be treated. If in any doubt, consult your doctor. An infusion to stimulate the appetite can be made from dandelion root. Chamomile, fennel, dill, aniseed, or lemon balm may settle an upset stomach caused by excess stomach acid—drink these teas after eating; they may also relieve gas.

Headaches

Lavender is used to reduce stress-related headaches. Drink an infusion of lavender flowers before meals three times a day. An infusion of valerian is used for tension headaches. Valerian and lavender in equal quantities may be used for a relaxing headache reliever. However, the most popular headache remedy is feverfew—a few leaves eaten several times a day help alleviate some migraines. The leaves can be eaten as a sandwich with bread, or used with other foods if desired. They can cause mouth irritation in some people, so try a small amount first to check. Tea can be made with dried feverfew leaves, in hot water—a half cup is recommended. If you suffer from migraines, take feverfew as for headaches. The effects for relieving migraine take some time to accumulate, so persevere.

Insomnia

We all suffer from disturbed sleep patterns at some time in our lives, and nothing can destroy the quality of life quicker than insomnia. Herbal remedies are a safe and healthy alternative to sleeping pills. They are non-addictive and gentle. The most commonly used, and probably the most effective, is chamomile. An infusion of 1 teaspoon of dried chamomile to 1 cup of hot water before bedtime is helpful. Lime flowers, or hop flowers, are used to help reduce any depression that accompanies insomnia. A tea made with mullein flowers can be helpful, as can passion flower and orange blossom if used in infusions. Another useful remedy to combat insomnia is a mixture of 2 parts skullcap, 2 parts passion flower, 1 part hops, 1 part valerian, and a tiny pinch of licorice—make an infusion of 2 teaspoons of the dried ingredients in 1 cup of hot water.

Stress

Herbal teas for relaxation are made with valerian, hops, passion flowers, or chamomile. To help restore nerves after a period of stress, take teas made with skullcap or ginseng. These teas all provide relaxants, and coffee, alcohol, and tobacco should be avoided while you are stressed, or recovering from stress, as they all stimulate the nervous system.

Drinks for Kids

Healthy drinks and kids can go together! Tempt them away from their usual sugary, fizzy, fare with this exciting selection of herbal tea drinks, based on tried-and-tested traditional recipes.

Apple *barley*

Serves 5

⅓ cup pearl barley
7½ cups boiling water
1 apple, peeled and sliced
Juice of ½ lemon
sugar to taste
1 oz dried lemon verbena
1 oz rosehip granules or crushed rosehips

Wash the barley and put it in a saucepan with 2½ cups of water. Bring to a boil, reduce the heat, and simmer for 15 minutes. Add the remaining water and other ingredients, except the herbs, to the pan, and boil until the liquid has reduced by half, about 15 minutes. Add the lemon verbena and rosehip granules or crushed rosehips, and simmer for 5 more minutes. Strain and cool. Refrigerate when cold. Serve on its own, or mixed half and half with hot water for a warm drink, or half and half with lemonade for a fizzy drink. Sweeten to taste.

TIP If you do not have time to make your own apple barley, make a cup of herbal tea using a recipe from this book, or a herbal teabag, and add a tablespoon of undiluted barley water in the flavor of your child's choice (e.g. apple, orange, lemon, mixed fruit). Serve hot or cold.

Old-fashioned *lemonade*

This traditional lemonade makes a great drink when mixed half and half with fizzy lemon-flavored drink or with ginger ale.

Serves 8

juice and grated rind of 2 oranges
juice and grated rind of 2 lemons
⅓ cup light-brown sugar
1 oz dried mallow
5 cups boiling water

Put all the ingredients in a large tea pot, jug, or other container, and pour over the water. Let stand for 30 minutes. Strain and rinse the lemon and orange rinds before putting in a container that will fit in the fridge where the lemonade should be chilled before serving over ice.
With Alcohol Add 1 measure (1½ Tbsp) fino sherry per half glass for a summery aperitif, or mix half and half with white wine.

Fruity *brose*

This simple fruit-and-herbal tea version of the adult drink, Athole Brose (see page 67), is great for children. Just follow the recipe for Athole Brose, and leave out the whisky.

Serves 6

1 apple, peeled, cored, and thinly
**   sliced**
¼ cup medium oatmeal
1 oz dried mullein
3½ cups boiling water
concentrated apple juice or honey
**   to sweeten**

Remember that children may require their brose to be sweetened by more honey than an adult would desire. This drink is also delicious cold, so alternatively refrigerate before serving. Oatmeal is nutritious and filling, so the drink really serves as a healthy snack as much as a refreshing drink.

Garnishes and Decorations for Drinks

- Sprigs of fresh herbs: mint, Italian parsley, cilantro, dill, chervil, basil.
- Herb (and other) edible flowers.
- Slices of lemon, lime, or orange slit to fit over the side of the glass, or put slices and wedges of citrus fruit in the glass or cup.
- Strips of twisted peel over the side of the glass.
- Thin strips of blanched orange or lemon peel. Cut as if for making orange marmalade. Put them in the base of the cup, glass, or tea pot.
- Slices of cucumber. Use peeled, with patterns cut into the peel, or unpeeled.
- Radishes with green tops cut to stick over side of glass.
- Sprigs of sugared currants (red, white, or black), or grapes, dipped in egg white, rolled in sifted confectioner's sugar, and dried in the pantry or on a warm shelf in the kitchen.
- Celery stalks with leaves.
- Cucumber sticks.

Toothpicks placed across the top of cups and glasses threaded with the following:
- Savory: Cherry tomatoes, fennel, celery, carrot, strips of peppers, or snow-peas.
- Sweet: Strawberry, pineapple chunks, papaya chunks, satsuma segments, or raspberries.

Cocktail paraphernalia:
- Iced glasses
- Iced and sugared or salted rims
- Cocktail umbrellas
- Glass cocktail rods
- Colorful straws

Sources *for Herbs*

Fresh herbs

Supermarkets, garden centers, general grocery stores (especially Asian), grocers, ethnic specialty stores such as delicatessens, food halls in department stores, street markets, and specialty herb stores, all sell fresh herbs. They are either prepacked or sold as growing herbs in pots.

Dried herbs

Available mainly from health-food shops and similar specialty stores such as apothecaries, some pharmacies, or some specialty grocery stores especially Asian. Also available by mail order.

US Sources

American Herb Association,
PO Box 1673 Nevada City, C A 95959.
Tel 916 265 9552. Fax 916 274 3140

Herb Directory of mail-order medical herbal products. More than 100 listings for herb products, supplies, containers, raw materials, plants, as well as fresh and dried herbs.

Herb Research Foundation,
1007 Pearl Street, Suite 200, Boulder, CO 80302.
Tel 303 449 2265. Fax 303 449 7849.

American Herbal Products Association,
Tel 301 951 3204.

American Botanical Council,
PO Box 201660, Austin, Texas 78720.
Tel 512 331 8868. Fax 512 331 1924.

UK Sources

G. Baldwin & Co.,
173 Walworth Road, London SE17 1RW.
Tel (0044) 171 703 5550. Fax (0044) 171 252 6264.
Email: sales@baldwins.co.uk

Neal's Yard Remedies,
31 King Street, Manchester M2 6AA.
Telephone (0044) 161 831 7875.
Fax (0044) 161 831 7873

The Herbal Apothecary,
103 High Street, Syston, Leicester LE7 1GQ.
Tel (0044) 116 2602690. Fax (0044) 116 2602757.

Index

Acknowledgments

The author would like to thank Roni Jay for all her invaluable research for this book.

The publishers would like to thank Janette Marshall for developing the recipes and valuable comments on the text.

Silver Sage at www.geocities.com
Dr. Leung's Newsletter at www.aylscorp.com
Horizon Herbs at www.chatlink.com
HERBS ONLINE at www.pacificnet.net
D. W. Reid at Coyote Creek Native Herbs

Picture Credits

The Publishers would like to thank the following for permission to reproduce copyright material: p. 7, ET Archive; p. 16, p. 32, p. 64, A-Z Botanical Ltd.